Little **BIG** Chats

Secrets and Surprises

by Jayneen Sanders

illustrated by Cherie Zamazing

Secrets and Surprises
Educate2Empower Publishing an imprint of
UpLoad Publishing Pty Ltd
Victoria Australia
www.upload.com.au

First published in 2021

Written by Jayneen Sanders
Illustrations by Cherie Zamazing

Jayneen Sanders asserts her right to be identified as the author of this work.
Cherie Zamazing asserts her right to be identified as the illustrator of this work.

Designed by Stephanie Spartels, Studio Spartels

ISBN: 9781761160271 (hbk) 9781761160134 (pbk)

A catalogue record for this
book is available from the
National Library of Australia

Disclaimer: The information in this book is advice only, written by the author based on
her advocacy in this area, and her experience working with children as a classroom teacher
and mother. The information is not meant to be a substitute for professional advice. If you
are concerned about a child's behavior seek professional help.

Using Little BIG Chats

The *Little BIG Chats* series has been written to assist parents, caregivers and educators to have open and age-appropriate conversations with young children around crucial, and yet at times, 'tough' topics. And what better way than using children's picture books! Some pages will have questions for your child to interact with and discuss. Feel free to use these questions and the Discussion Questions provided on page 19 of this book to help you assist your child with the topic being explored. Stop at any time to unpack the text together; and try to follow your child's lead wherever that conversation may take you! So, please, get comfy and start some empowering 'chats' around some BIG topics with your child.

The Body Safety titles should ideally be read in the following order:
*Consent, My Safety Network, My Early Warning Signs,
Private Parts are Private,* and *Secrets and Surprises.*
The remaining titles can be read in any order.

Meet the Little **BIG** Chats KIDS

Theodore

Asha

Ardie

Tom

Jun

Jamie

Belle

Lisa

Maisy

Tilly

Maya

Ben

Hi! I'm Lisa.
Today we're learning about the difference between secrets and surprises.

Secrets and surprises
are very different.

Secrets might
NEVER be told.

But surprises will
ALWAYS be told.

Last year we had a party
for my grandma.

It was a surprise!

Everyone knew
about the party,
but Grandma didn't.

So, on Grandma's birthday,
she got a big surprise!

The party was so much fun!

In my family, we don't keep secrets.
We only keep happy surprises
because they will ALWAYS be told.

WHAT IS THE BIGGEST SURPRISE YOU HAVE EVER HAD?

Secrets are different to surprises.

Sometimes a person might ask you to keep a secret.

If that happens, say, 'I don't keep secrets. I only keep happy surprises because they will ALWAYS be told.'

I don't keep secrets.
I only keep happy
surprises because they
will ALWAYS be told.

Sometimes a person might ask you to keep a secret that makes you feel unsafe or scared.

If that happens, you can say, 'I don't keep secrets. I only keep happy surprises because they will ALWAYS be told.'

I don't keep secrets.
I only keep happy
surprises because they
will ALWAYS be told.

Then go quickly and tell a trusted grown-up on your Safety Network.

Secrets that make you feel unsafe or scared should never ever be kept.

WHAT SHOULD YOU DO
IF SOMEONE ASKS YOU
TO KEEP A SECRET?

Remember!

It's okay to keep happy surprises because they will always be told.

DISCUSSION QUESTIONS
for Parents, Caregivers and Educators

The following Discussion Questions are intended as a guide, and can be used to initiate open, age-appropriate and empowering conversations with your child.

This book introduces children to the difference between secrets and surprises. Perpetrators will often ask children to keep abuse secret – children understanding that they don't keep secrets only happy surprises because they will always be told, is part of their 'toolkit' to help keep them safe.

Page 5
Introduce Lisa. Ask, 'What do you think a secret is? What do you think a surprise is?'

Pages 6-7
Ask, 'Have you ever been asked to keep a secret that made you feel unsafe or uncomfortable? What did you do?' Note: if a child begins to disclose abuse, seek professional help as soon as possible. However, at the immediate time of disclosure, listen, stay calm and make no promises of the abuse stopping. There is extensive information on disclosures in the book 'Body Safety Education' by Jayneen Sanders.

Ask, 'Have you ever been asked to keep a surprise? What was it? Was the surprise told?'

Pages 8-9
Ask, 'Have you ever had or been to a surprise birthday party? Would you like to tell me about it? Was everyone excited about the surprise?'

Pages 10-11
Ask, 'In our family is it a good idea to use the word "surprises" rather than "secrets"? Why do you say that? How does everyone look in this picture?'

Pages 12-13
Say, 'Let's practice saying, "I don't keep secrets. I only keep happy surprises because they will always be told."' Note: it will be quite difficult to remove the word 'secrets' out of everyone's vocabulary (including family) but it's important that children understand a secret is often asked to be kept, whereas a 'surprise' will be told.

Pages 14-15
Ask, 'What does it mean when the boy puts his hand to his mouth like this (show your child). That's right! He is asking Lisa to keep a secret about the sweets. Do you think Lisa feels happy about keeping the secret? How can you tell? Has anyone asked you to keep a secret that made you feel unsafe or scared?' Note: See information on disclosures in Discussion Questions pages 6–7.

Pages 16-17
Ask, 'What should you do if someone asks you to keep a secret that makes you feel unsafe, uncomfortable or scared?' Praise your child's answer which should be, 'Tell a trusted adult on my Safety Network straightaway.' Note: encourage your child to decide on three to five adults that they trust and help them form a Safety Network. (See the book 'My Safety Network' included in the Little BIG Chats series.)

Page 18
Say, 'Look! Lisa has a happy surprise. What is it? Do you think Lisa's family kept the happy surprise for a very long time or for just a short time? How do you think Lisa is feeling right now?'

For more books on secrets and surprises, see Jayneen Sanders' children's books 'My Body! What I Say Goes!', 'ABC of Body Safety and Consent' and 'Some Secrets Should Never Be Kept'.

Little BIG Chats

A series of 12 little books to help kids unpack BIG topics

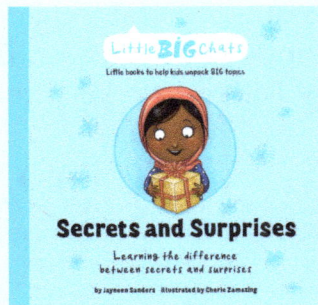

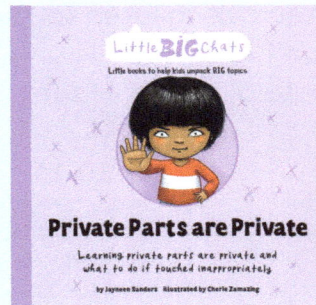

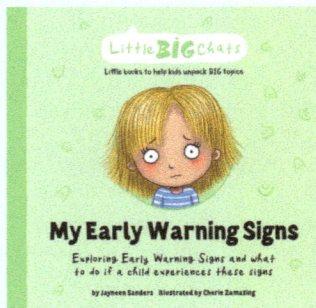

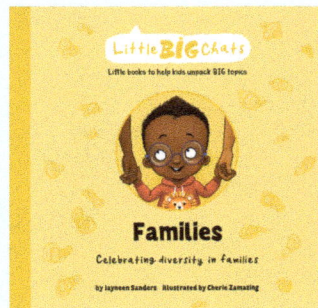

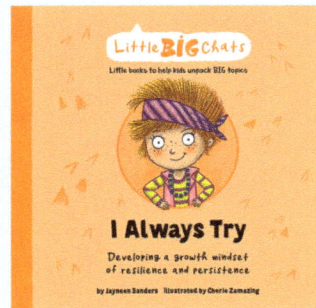

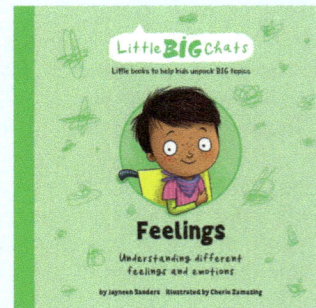

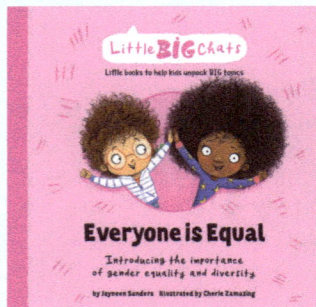

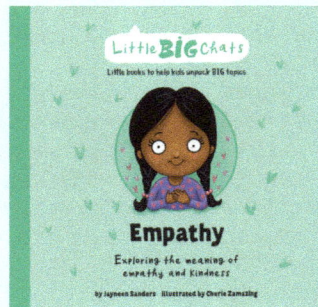

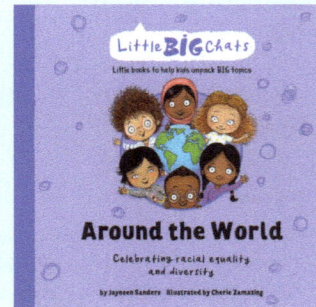

Consent
Introducing consent and body boundaries
by Jayneen Sanders   Illustrated by Cherie Zamazing

Secrets and Surprises
Learning the difference between secrets and surprises
by Jayneen Sanders   Illustrated by Cherie Zamazing

Private Parts are Private
Learning private parts are private and what to do if touched inappropriately
by Jayneen Sanders   Illustrated by Cherie Zamazing

My Safety Network
Introducing a Safety Network (3 to 5 trusted adults a child can go to if they feel unsafe)
by Jayneen Sanders   Illustrated by Cherie Zamazing

My Early Warning Signs
Exploring Early Warning Signs and what to do if a child experiences these signs
by Jayneen Sanders   Illustrated by Cherie Zamazing

Families
Celebrating diversity in families
by Jayneen Sanders   Illustrated by Cherie Zamazing

I Always Try
Developing a growth mindset of resilience and persistence
by Jayneen Sanders   Illustrated by Cherie Zamazing

Feelings
Understanding different feelings and emotions
by Jayneen Sanders   Illustrated by Cherie Zamazing

Everyone is Equal
Introducing the importance of gender equality and diversity
by Jayneen Sanders   Illustrated by Cherie Zamazing

Empathy
Exploring the meaning of empathy and kindness
by Jayneen Sanders   Illustrated by Cherie Zamazing

Mindfulness
Exploring the importance of mindfulness and learning calming skills
by Jayneen Sanders   Illustrated by Cherie Zamazing

Around the World
Celebrating racial equality and diversity
by Jayneen Sanders   Illustrated by Cherie Zamazing

www.ingramcontent.com/pod-product-compliance
Lightning Source LLC
Chambersburg PA
CBHW040002040426
42337CB00032B/5203